The Mess That We Made

T0112964

Written by Michelle Lord   Illustrated by Julia Blattman

FLASHLIGHT PRESS

Flash
Light
PRESS

For my husband,
the original recycler.
And for the children,
"Seas" the day — do your part
to protect our oceans! –ML

To my parents who always
supported me. –JB

Paperback edition copyright © 2024 by Flashlight Press
Copyright © 2020 by Flashlight Press
Text copyright © 2020 by Michelle Lord
Illustrations copyright © 2020 by Julia Blattman

All rights reserved, including the right of reproduction,
in whole or in part, in any form. Cataloging-in-Publication data
is available from the Library of Congress.

Printed in China on eco-friendly paper, and in compliance with the ISO 14001
environmental management system. Paperback edition 1st printing, August 2024.

8x8 Paperback 9781962269001 · Hardcover 9781947277144 · ePDF 9781947277151
EPUB 9781947277168 · KF8 9781947277175 · Audiobook: 9781947277601 · Read-along Audio: 9781947277557

Editor: Shari Dash Greenspan · Graphic Design: The Virtual Paintbrush
This book was typeset in Omorika. The illustrations were created digitally.

Distributed by IPG · Flashlight Press · 527 Empire Blvd., Brooklyn, NY 11225 · FlashlightPress.com

THIS is the mess that we made.

These are the fish
that swim in the mess that we made.

This is the seal
that eats the fish
that swim in the mess that we made.

This is the net
that catches the seal,
that eats the fish
that swim in the mess that we made.

This is the boat of welded steel,
that dumps the net,
that catches the seal,
that eats the fish
that swim in the mess that we made.

This is the current that swirls through the bay,
that rocks the boat of welded steel,
that dumps the net,
that catches the seal,
that eats the fish
that swim in the mess that we made.

This is the turtle, green and gray,
that rides the current through the bay,

that rocks the boat of welded steel,
that dumps the net,
that catches the seal,
that eats the fish
that swim in the mess that we made.

This is the plastic, thrown away,
that traps the turtle, green and gray,
that rides the current through the bay,

that rocks the boat of welded steel,
that dumps the net,
that catches the seal,
that eats the fish
that swim in the mess that we made.

This is the landfill, growing each day,
that spills the plastic, thrown away,
that traps the turtle, green and gray,
that rides the current through the bay,
that rocks the boat of welded steel,

LANDFILL

that dumps the net,
that catches the seal,
that eats the fish
that swim in the mess that we made.

We are the people at work and at play,
that stuff the landfill, growing each day,
that spills the plastic thrown away,
that traps the turtle, green and gray,
that rides the current through the bay,
that rocks the boat of welded steel,
that dumps the net,
that catches the seal,
that eats the fish
that swim in the mess that we made.

Look at the mess that we made.

BUT... we are the ones who can save the day,
reduce our waste at work and at play,
recycle the plastic thrown away,

to shrink the landfill without delay.

We rescue the turtle, green and gray,

and haul the garbage from the bay.

We protest the boat of welded steel,
collect the nets
and free the seal,
that eats the fish...

that swim in the ocean that WE save!

This is the mess that we made.

Discovered in 1997 by marine researcher Charles Moore, the **Great Pacific Garbage Patch** consists of two huge, growing masses of trash known as the Eastern and Western Garbage Patches. The Western Patch lies near Japan, and the Eastern Patch lies between Hawaii and California. In 2018, the Eastern Patch alone weighed more than 43,000 cars, and was more than twice the size of Texas or three times the size of France.

Almost all of the trash in the Great Pacific Garbage Patch is plastic. Why so much plastic? Because plastic doesn't biodegrade like wood or plants. Instead, sunlight and waves very slowly break plastic into smaller and smaller pieces.

These are the fish... This is the seal...

Scientists group plastic by size. The smallest pieces are called **microplastics**, and there are trillions of these particles in the ocean. They make the water in the Garbage Patch look like cloudy soup.

Microplastics get eaten by fish and other small sea creatures. When larger marine animals like seals eat these fish, the microplastic moves up the food chain. And when we eat these fish and shellfish, the chemicals from the plastic can enter our bodies and make us sick.

The bulk of the Garbage Patch is composed of larger pieces of plastic called **mesoplastics**, **macroplastics**, and **megaplastics**. These include food containers, bottles, and lids, and fishing gear like buckets, ropes, and nets.

This is the turtle... This is the plastic...

A sea turtle's favorite food is jellyfish. But floating plastic bags look a lot like jellyfish! When turtles swallow plastic bags, their digestive systems get blocked, which can be deadly. A study in 2015 found that 52% of sea turtles and 90% of seabirds have eaten some form of plastic.

When young sea turtles get caught in plastic six-pack rings, their shells grow misshapen, their lungs cannot develop properly, and they can die. When birds get caught in plastic rings, then can have trouble flying. If they can't fly, they can't find food and they can be attacked.

🐢 Bring reusable bags to grocery stores instead of taking single-use plastic bags. Cut the loops on anything that might entangle marine life before you dispose of it.

This is the landfill...

How are landfills created? We throw our trash into garbage bins. Then trucks collect it and dump it into landfills. Because most of the plastic we use does not get recycled, plastics and Styrofoam make up 30% of the landfill volume in the US.

But storms can blow or wash trash out of open landfills into the ocean. Rain can wash trash from sidewalks and streets into sewers or rivers where it can be carried out to sea. Ultimately, 10% of the plastic dumped into landfills ends up in the ocean. If things continue the way they are now, by 2050, all of the plastic in the ocean will weigh more than all of the fish in the ocean!

🐢 Don't litter – always dispose of your trash in proper receptacles or recycling bins.

CALLS TO ACTION

Sources consulted for this section can be found on our website FlashlightPress.com

This is the net... This is the boat...

Fishing nets make up more than half of the large plastic objects in the Garbage Patch. Called ghost nets, these are loose nets that have been lost or purposely dumped into the sea. Sadly, ghost nets continue to float around in the ocean, endangering fish, turtles, seals and other mammals, and coral.

Cargo ships are another source of marine trash. More than 1,500 shipping containers get washed into the ocean every year during bad weather. In 1997, a shipping container of LEGO® products went overboard in the Atlantic Ocean, and LEGO toys washed ashore for decades in England, Ireland, Australia, and Texas.

How did the LEGO pieces travel so far? They were carried by currents.

This is the current...

Currents are the movements of water through the ocean. When currents meet, they form large circular systems called gyres (pronounced like the first syllable of "gyroscope"). Most of the trash in the ocean gets pulled into the five main gyres around the world, forming swirling masses of ocean garbage patches.

Trash from the west coast of North America can take up to 6 years to get trapped in the Great Pacific Garbage Patch; trash from Asia's east coast gets trapped in about a year.

The oldest piece of plastic found in the Garbage Patch during a 2015 study by The Ocean Cleanup organization was from 1977. It had been floating around for almost 40 years!

We are the people...

Did you know that people around the world buy **one million plastic bottles every minute** and use **more than half a billion plastic straws every day**?! In 2016, Americans threw away 25 billion Styrofoam cups!

World-wide, eight million metric tons of discarded plastic items enter our oceans each year – including huge quantities of single-use plastic bags, disposable cutlery, and food packaging – adding to the estimated 150 million metric tons that already pollute our marine environments.

Look at the mess that we made.

No one knows exactly how much trash is in the Great Pacific Garbage Patch, since it's too large to measure and because heavier trash can sink a few inches or even a few yards underwater. Oceanographers recently found that about 70% of marine trash sinks to the bottom of the ocean. The seabed beneath the Garbage Patch may be an underwater trash heap.

How long does it take for the things we use to decompose? Wool socks: 1–5 years, batteries: 100 years, disposable diapers: 400 years, plastic bottles: 450 years, toothbrushes: 500 years, fishing line: 600 years, and plastic bags: up to 1,000 years.

Use reusable or recyclable straws, or drink straight from the cup. When you need to use disposable cutlery, cups, or plates, try to use ones made from biodegradable materials such as paper, bamboo, or plant starch.

 Drink from reusable water bottles.

OCEAN POLLUTION and CALLS TO ACTION

But we are the ones who can save the day...

Minimizing our use of disposable plastic is one of the best ways to keep the Garbage Patch from growing. What can we do? Reduce! Reuse! Recycle! Reducing the amount of things we buy – especially plastic – and reusing the items we already own, will produce less waste. Recycling properly will send less garbage to landfills so less will end up in the oceans.

Reduce by starting a home garden. Growing food at home saves on single-use packaging. Shop for second-hand clothing instead of buying new. Eat at restaurants that avoid Styrofoam to-go containers, or bring your own containers for leftovers. **Reuse** or repurpose things rather than throwing them away. For example, you can use a milk jug to water your plants instead of buying a new watering can. **Recycle** paper, glass, metal, and plastic. Recycle outgrown clothing by donating it.

shrink the landfill...

Around the world, some landfills are being reclaimed as parks and nature reserves. In Virginia, USA, workers compacted layers of solid waste with clean soil to create Mount Trashmore Park. Near Tel Aviv, Israel, a landfill once known as Garbage Mountain was transformed into an environmental park called Ariel Sharon Park. A landfill in Hong Kong became a multi-purpose playground called Sai Tso Wan Recreation Ground.

Volunteer for clean-ups in your area to remove trash from beaches, rivers, lakes, and your neighborhood. Visit a recycling center or landfill with your class or family to see for yourself where our plastic ends up. Even a small action like using a lunchbox and reusable containers instead of a disposable bag and baggies can make a difference.

rescue... haul... protest... collect... free...

The Great Pacific Garbage Patch is so far from any country's coastline that no nation will take responsibility or pay for cleaning it up. However, innovative people, organizations, and companies around the globe are working on ways to remove plastic from oceans, prevent plastic from getting into oceans in the first place, improve recycling methods, and invent biodegradable substitutes for plastic.

Fight for change – not with fists but with words. Join a peaceful protest against ocean pollution with your family, friends, or classmates. Stop plastic at the source! Write to corporations to ask them to stop producing single-use plastic packaging or products. Ask politicians to pass laws limiting or ending production of non-recyclable and single-use plastics, to ban the dumping of ghost nets, and to help clean up our oceans.

that swim in the ocean that we save!

Our oceans provide humans with food, oxygen, renewable energy, jobs, and recreation. They help regulate our climate by absorbing carbon dioxide, and affect our weather and drinking water as part of the water cycle.

Even if we don't live near one, oceans are a crucial part of life on Earth. It's important that we do our best to keep them healthy! Each and every one of us can make a difference to save our seas.

Educate yourself and learn as much as you can. Read books and articles about the Great Pacific Garbage Patch and ocean pollution. Visit FlashlightPress.com for links to organizations and innovative companies that are working to clean up our oceans.